CONTENTS

Tailoring Estate Planning to Life's Late

CHAPTER 1: INTRODUCTION TO ESTATE PLANNING

Estate planning is not merely a legal or financial exercise; it's a deeply personal and responsible act that allows individuals to exert control over their assets, provide for their loved ones, and ensure their wishes are honored both during their lifetime and after they pass away. In this chapter, we will explore the multifaceted nature of estate planning, its importance, and the fundamental principles that underpin this critical aspect of financial management.

Understanding Estate Planning: Beyond the Basics

Estate planning is often misunderstood as simply the process of drafting a will. While a will is indeed a central component of estate planning, the concept encompasses a far broader range of considerations. At its core, estate planning involves the strategic management and distribution of assets, the protection of wealth, the minimization of taxes and expenses, and the provision for the care of oneself and loved ones in the event of incapacity or death.

To delve deeper, estate planning is about:

- **Asset Protection**: Shielding assets from potential creditors, lawsuits, and other liabilities to preserve wealth for intended beneficiaries.

- **Tax Minimization**: Structuring estate plans to minimize tax liabilities, including estate taxes, gift taxes, and income taxes, thereby maximizing the value of the assets passed on to heirs.

- **Family Harmony**: Promoting harmony among family members by clearly outlining how assets will be distributed and minimizing the potential for disputes or conflicts.

- **Healthcare Planning**: Ensuring that individuals have a say in their medical care and treatment preferences, even if they become incapacitated, through advance healthcare directives and healthcare proxies.

- **Legacy Preservation**: Preserving one's values, beliefs, and legacy by supporting charitable causes, passing on family traditions, and leaving a lasting impact on future generations.

Why Estate Planning Matters: Real-Life Scenarios

To illustrate the significance of estate planning, consider the following scenarios:

1. **Family Disputes**: Without a clear estate plan, family members may disagree about how assets should be distributed, leading to lengthy and costly legal battles that can strain relationships.

2. **Tax Consequences**: Failing to engage in proper estate planning can result in significant tax liabilities, diminishing the value of the estate and reducing the inheritance received by beneficiaries.

3. **Incapacity Planning**: In the absence of advance directives and powers of attorney, decisions regarding medical treatment and financial matters may be left to courts or appointed guardians, who may not act in accordance with the individual's wishes.

4. **Asset Protection**: Without proper planning, assets may be vulnerable to creditors, lawsuits, or imprudent

financial decisions, jeopardizing the financial security of heirs and beneficiaries.

The Components of Estate Planning: Building Blocks for Success

A well-rounded estate plan typically comprises various components, each serving a specific purpose in achieving the individual's goals and objectives. These components may include:

- **Last Will and Testament**: A legal document that outlines how assets will be distributed upon death and appoints guardians for minor children, among other provisions.

- **Trusts**: Legal arrangements that hold assets on behalf of beneficiaries, providing flexibility, privacy, and potential tax benefits while avoiding probate.

- **Powers of Attorney**: Documents that authorize designated individuals to make financial and healthcare decisions on behalf of the grantor in the event of incapacity.

- **Advance Healthcare Directives**: Instructions that specify an individual's preferences for medical treatment and appoint a healthcare proxy to make healthcare decisions if the individual is unable to do so.

- **Beneficiary Designations**: Designations that dictate who will receive assets from certain accounts or insurance policies upon the account holder's death, bypassing probate.

- **Letter of Instruction**: A non-binding document that provides guidance to executors, trustees, and beneficiaries regarding the administration of the estate, funeral arrangements, and other matters.

Collaborating with Estate Planning Professionals: Expert Guidance for Peace of Mind

Given the complexity and legal implications of estate planning, seeking guidance from experienced professionals is highly advisable. Estate planning attorneys, financial advisors, tax experts, and other professionals can offer invaluable insights, tailor strategies to individual needs, and ensure that estate plans are legally sound and effective in achieving desired outcomes.

Conclusion: Empowering Individuals through Thoughtful Planning

In conclusion, estate planning is an essential aspect of financial management that empowers individuals to take control of their assets, provide for their loved ones, and leave a lasting legacy. By embracing the principles of estate planning and crafting comprehensive plans tailored to their unique circumstances, individuals can navigate life's uncertainties with confidence and ensure that their wishes are honored, both now and in the future. Throughout this book, we will delve deeper into the intricacies of estate planning, providing practical guidance, real-world examples, and expert insights to help readers navigate this vital aspect of their financial journey.

CHAPTER 2: UNDERSTANDING THE BASICS OF ESTATE PLANNING

Estate planning is a multifaceted process that goes beyond mere asset distribution; it encompasses a strategic approach to managing one's affairs, protecting assets, and ensuring that personal wishes are fulfilled both during life and after death. In this chapter, we will delve into the foundational principles and intricate details of estate planning, offering readers a comprehensive understanding of its essential components and significance in financial management.

The Essence of Estate Planning

At its core, estate planning is about taking control of one's financial and personal affairs to ensure they align with individual goals and values. It involves making decisions today to safeguard assets, provide for loved ones, and preserve one's legacy for future generations. While often associated with the elderly or the wealthy, estate planning is relevant for individuals of all ages and financial backgrounds.

The Four Pillars of Estate Planning

Estate planning rests on four fundamental pillars:

1. **Asset Management and Distribution**: Determining how assets will be managed and distributed upon death,

including the allocation of financial resources, real estate, investments, business interests, and personal possessions.

2. **Incapacity Planning**: Planning for the possibility of incapacity due to illness, injury, or advanced age, and ensuring that trusted individuals are empowered to make financial and healthcare decisions on behalf of the incapacitated person.

3. **Tax Mitigation Strategies**: Implementing strategies to minimize tax liabilities, including estate taxes, gift taxes, and income taxes, thereby preserving the maximum value of assets for intended beneficiaries.

4. **Legacy Preservation**: Preserving one's values, beliefs, and personal legacy through philanthropy, charitable giving, and the transmission of family traditions, stories, and values to future generations.

Key Components of Estate Planning

A comprehensive estate plan typically includes the following components:

1. **Last Will and Testament**: A legal document that specifies how assets will be distributed upon death, appoints guardians for minor children, and nominates executors to oversee the administration of the estate.

2. **Trusts**: Legal arrangements that hold assets on behalf of beneficiaries, providing flexibility, control, and privacy while potentially minimizing estate taxes and avoiding probate.

3. **Powers of Attorney**: Documents that designate trusted individuals to make financial and healthcare decisions on behalf of the grantor in the event of incapacity.

4. **Advance Healthcare Directives**: Instructions that express an individual's wishes regarding medical treatment and appoint a healthcare proxy to make

healthcare decisions if the individual is unable to do so.

5. **Beneficiary Designations**: Designations that dictate who will receive assets from certain accounts or insurance policies upon the account holder's death, bypassing probate.

6. **Letter of Instruction**: A non-binding document that provides guidance to executors, trustees, and beneficiaries regarding the administration of the estate, funeral arrangements, and other matters.

Factors Influencing Estate Planning

Several factors may influence an individual's estate planning decisions, including:

- **Family Dynamics**: Understanding family relationships, dynamics, and potential conflicts can help tailor estate plans to promote harmony and minimize disputes among beneficiaries.

- **Asset Composition**: The types of assets owned, such as real estate, investments, retirement accounts, and business interests, will influence the structure and strategies of the estate plan.

- **Tax Implications**: Estate and gift taxes, as well as income taxes, can significantly impact the value of assets transferred to heirs. Proper planning can help minimize tax liabilities and maximize the inheritance received by beneficiaries.

- **State Laws**: Estate planning laws vary by state, so it's crucial to understand the legal requirements and implications specific to your jurisdiction when drafting your estate plan.

Collaborating with Estate Planning Professionals

Given the complexity and legal implications of estate planning, seeking guidance from experienced professionals is highly advisable. Estate planning attorneys, financial advisors, tax experts, and other professionals can offer invaluable insights, tailor strategies to individual needs, and ensure that estate plans are legally sound and effective in achieving desired outcomes.

Conclusion

In conclusion, estate planning is a vital component of financial management that empowers individuals to protect their assets, provide for their loved ones, and preserve their legacy for future generations. By understanding the foundational principles, key components, and influencing factors of estate planning, individuals can navigate this complex process with clarity and confidence, ensuring that their wishes are honored and their goals are achieved. In the subsequent chapters, we will explore specific aspects of estate planning in greater detail, providing practical guidance and expert insights to help readers develop comprehensive and effective estate plans tailored to their unique circumstances.

CHAPTER 3: SETTING YOUR GOALS: WHAT DO YOU WANT TO ACHIEVE?

Estate planning is a journey that begins with a clear understanding of what you want to accomplish. Your goals will serve as the guiding principles behind every decision you make in crafting your estate plan. In this chapter, we will delve deeply into the significance of setting goals in estate planning, explore various common objectives individuals aim to achieve, and provide comprehensive guidance on how to establish personalized goals that truly reflect your values, priorities, and aspirations.

Understanding the Fundamental Role of Goal Setting

Setting goals is the cornerstone of effective estate planning for several compelling reasons:

1. **Clarity and Direction**: Establishing specific, measurable goals provides you with a clear direction, enabling you to focus your efforts and resources on achieving desired outcomes.

2. **Alignment with Values**: Your estate planning goals should resonate with your core values, beliefs, and aspirations, ensuring that your plan reflects who you are and what matters most to you.

3. **Conflict Prevention**: Clearly defined goals can help prevent potential conflicts among family members by providing transparency and clarity regarding your intentions and wishes.

4. **Assessment of Success**: Goals serve as benchmarks against which you can measure the success of your estate plan, enabling you to evaluate whether your plan is effectively achieving the outcomes you desire.

Exploring Common Goals in Estate Planning

While estate planning goals are deeply personal and vary from one individual to another, certain objectives are commonly pursued by many people:

1. **Asset Protection**: Safeguarding your assets from potential risks, such as lawsuits, creditors, or divorce settlements, to preserve your wealth for yourself and your beneficiaries.

2. **Providing for Loved Ones**: Ensuring that your loved ones are provided for financially and emotionally, including spouses, children, grandchildren, and other dependents.

3. **Tax Efficiency**: Minimizing tax liabilities, including estate taxes, gift taxes, and income taxes, to maximize the value of assets transferred to heirs and beneficiaries.

4. **Avoiding Probate**: Avoiding or minimizing the probate process to streamline the administration of your estate, maintain privacy, and reduce costs and delays.

5. **Family Harmony**: Promoting harmony among family members by addressing potential conflicts, communicating openly about estate planning decisions, and fostering understanding and acceptance of your plan.

6. **Philanthropy and Legacy**: Supporting charitable causes and leaving a lasting legacy by incorporating

philanthropic giving into your estate plan.

7. **Healthcare Planning**: Ensuring that your healthcare wishes are honored and that trusted individuals are empowered to make medical decisions on your behalf if you become incapacitated.

Establishing Personalized Goals

To develop personalized estate planning goals that truly reflect your values and aspirations, consider the following steps:

1. **Self-Reflection**: Take time to reflect on your values, beliefs, and priorities, and consider how you want to be remembered and the legacy you wish to leave behind.

2. **Family Dynamics**: Evaluate family relationships, dynamics, and potential areas of conflict to tailor your estate plan in a way that promotes harmony and addresses the needs of all family members.

3. **Financial Assessment**: Assess your financial situation, including assets, liabilities, income, expenses, and future financial needs, to determine the most effective strategies for achieving your goals.

4. **Consultation with Professionals**: Seek guidance from experienced estate planning professionals, such as attorneys, financial advisors, and tax experts, to explore available options and develop strategies that align with your objectives.

Revisiting and Updating Goals

Estate planning goals are not static; they may evolve over time in response to changes in personal circumstances, family dynamics, financial situations, or legal considerations. It's essential to revisit and reassess your goals regularly to ensure that your estate plan remains relevant, effective, and aligned with your current priorities and aspirations.

Conclusion

In conclusion, setting clear and personalized goals is a critical first step in estate planning, providing the foundation upon which your entire plan will be built. By establishing specific objectives that resonate with your values and aspirations, you can create a comprehensive estate plan that reflects your wishes, promotes family harmony, and achieves your desired outcomes. In the subsequent chapters, we will delve deeper into various strategies and techniques for achieving specific estate planning goals, offering practical guidance and expert insights to help you navigate this important journey with confidence and clarity.

CHAPTER 4: ASSESSING YOUR ASSETS AND LIABILITIES: A COMPREHENSIVE ANALYSIS

In estate planning, a meticulous assessment of your assets and liabilities serves as the bedrock upon which you'll build a robust plan to safeguard your wealth and provide for your loved ones. This chapter delves into the intricate process of evaluating your financial landscape, exploring the depths of your assets and liabilities, and strategizing to optimize your estate plan based on this comprehensive analysis.

The Significance of Asset and Liability Assessment

1. **Holistic Financial Understanding**: By conducting a thorough assessment of your assets and liabilities, you gain a holistic understanding of your financial position. This insight empowers you to make informed decisions about wealth management, asset protection, and distribution planning.

2. **Strategic Decision-Making**: Understanding the composition and value of your assets allows you to

make strategic decisions that align with your estate planning goals. It enables you to identify opportunities for optimization and areas that may require attention or mitigation.

3. **Wealth Preservation and Distribution**: A clear assessment of your assets and liabilities forms the basis for determining how best to preserve and distribute your wealth to your intended beneficiaries. It helps ensure that your estate plan reflects your wishes and achieves your desired outcomes.

4. **Risk Management**: Assessing liabilities enables you to identify potential risks and liabilities that could impact your estate's value. By understanding these risks, you can implement strategies to mitigate them and protect your assets from potential threats.

Types of Assets to Consider

1. **Real Estate**: Evaluate the value and ownership structure of all real estate holdings, including primary residences, vacation homes, rental properties, and investment properties. Consider factors such as market value, rental income, and potential capital gains tax implications.

2. **Financial Assets**: Assess the value and composition of financial assets, including cash, savings accounts, investment portfolios, retirement accounts, and other securities. Analyze investment performance, risk exposure, and liquidity to optimize asset allocation strategies.

3. **Business Interests**: If you own business interests, evaluate their value, profitability, and liquidity. Consider factors such as ownership percentages, succession planning, and potential implications for estate taxes and family dynamics.

4. **Personal Property**: Take inventory of valuable personal

possessions, such as vehicles, jewelry, artwork, antiques, and collectibles. Consider appraisal values, sentimental significance, and potential estate tax implications for high-value items.

5. **Digital Assets**: Assess the value and accessibility of digital assets, including online accounts, digital files, cryptocurrencies, and intellectual property rights. Develop strategies for managing and transferring digital assets in accordance with your wishes and legal considerations.

Liabilities to Evaluate

1. **Debts and Obligations**: Identify and quantify all outstanding debts and obligations, including mortgages, loans, credit card debt, and tax liabilities. Assess interest rates, repayment terms, and potential implications for estate liquidity and distribution planning.

2. **Tax Liabilities**: Evaluate potential tax liabilities, including income taxes, property taxes, estate taxes, and gift taxes. Consider tax-efficient strategies for minimizing tax exposure and maximizing wealth preservation for your beneficiaries.

3. **Insurance Coverage**: Review existing insurance policies, including life insurance, disability insurance, and long-term care insurance. Assess coverage amounts, policy terms, and beneficiaries to ensure alignment with your estate planning goals and objectives.

Strategies for Optimizing Your Estate Plan

1. **Asset Protection**: Implement asset protection strategies, such as irrevocable trusts, family limited partnerships, or asset titling techniques, to shield assets from creditors, lawsuits, and other potential threats.

2. **Tax Planning**: Utilize tax planning strategies, such as

lifetime gifting, charitable giving, or estate freezing techniques, to minimize estate taxes and maximize the value of assets transferred to your heirs.

3. **Debt Management**: Develop a plan for managing and reducing outstanding debts, prioritizing high-interest liabilities and implementing repayment strategies to minimize financial burdens on your estate and beneficiaries.

4. **Insurance Review**: Conduct a comprehensive review of insurance coverage to ensure adequate protection for your estate and loved ones. Consider factors such as coverage amounts, policy terms, beneficiary designations, and potential tax implications.

Conclusion

Assessing your assets and liabilities is a foundational step in estate planning, providing critical insights that inform strategic decision-making and plan optimization. By conducting a comprehensive analysis of your financial landscape, you can identify opportunities for wealth preservation, risk mitigation, and tax optimization, ensuring that your estate plan aligns with your goals and objectives. In the subsequent chapters, we will delve deeper into various estate planning strategies and techniques, offering practical guidance and expert insights to help you navigate the complexities of estate planning with confidence and clarity.

CHAPTER 5: THE IMPORTANCE OF WILLS IN ESTATE PLANNING

Wills stand as the cornerstone of estate planning, embodying the final wishes and directives of an individual for the distribution of their assets and the protection of their loved ones after their passing. In this chapter, we will delve deeply into the profound significance of wills in estate planning, examining their multifaceted roles, essential components, and the critical importance of meticulous drafting and periodic review.

The Foundational Role of Wills

1. **Guardianship Designations**: Perhaps one of the most crucial aspects of a will is the ability to designate guardians for minor children. This provision ensures that parents have a say in who will care for their children if both parents pass away prematurely, offering peace of mind and security for the well-being of their offspring.

2. **Asset Distribution**: Wills serve as the primary mechanism for expressing how a person's assets should be distributed among beneficiaries. From financial assets to sentimental possessions, a will provides a clear roadmap for the allocation of wealth, minimizing the potential for disputes among heirs.

3. **Executor Appointment**: By nominating an executor, individuals can entrust the responsibility of managing their estate to a trusted individual. This executor will oversee the administration of the will, including asset inventory, debt settlement, and distribution of assets according to the testator's wishes.

4. **Probate Streamlining**: While probate can be a complex and time-consuming process, a well-drafted will can streamline the proceedings by providing clear instructions for asset distribution. This clarity reduces the burden on the court and facilitates the efficient transfer of assets to beneficiaries.

5. **Legacy Preservation**: Beyond the logistical aspects, wills serve as a testament to a person's values, beliefs, and desires for their legacy. Through specific bequests, charitable donations, or other provisions, individuals can ensure that their values endure beyond their lifetime.

Essential Components of a Comprehensive Will

1. **Testator Identification**: A will should begin with the identification of the testator, including their full legal name, date of birth, and place of residence. This ensures clarity and helps prevent any confusion regarding the identity of the person making the will.

2. **Executor Nomination**: The appointment of an executor is crucial, as this individual will carry out the instructions outlined in the will. It's essential to choose someone who is trustworthy, responsible, and capable of managing the estate's affairs impartially.

3. **Asset Distribution Plan**: The heart of the will lies in its provisions for asset distribution. This section should clearly outline how assets will be distributed among beneficiaries, specifying each beneficiary's share and any conditions or restrictions on inheritance.

4. **Guardianship Designations**: For parents with minor children, the will should designate guardians who will assume responsibility for the care and upbringing of the children in the event of the parents' death. Thoughtful consideration should be given to the guardians' suitability and willingness to take on this role.

5. **Contingency Plans**: A comprehensive will includes provisions for unforeseen circumstances, such as the death or incapacity of beneficiaries or executors. Contingency plans ensure that the estate's affairs are managed effectively, even in unexpected situations.

The Importance of Regular Review and Updating

While drafting a will is a significant step in estate planning, its effectiveness hinges on its relevance to the testator's current circumstances and intentions. Therefore, regular review and updating of the will are paramount. Life events, changes in financial status, and evolving family dynamics can all necessitate revisions to the will to ensure that it accurately reflects the testator's wishes.

Conclusion

In conclusion, wills play a central role in estate planning, providing a legal framework for asset distribution, guardianship designations, and executor appointments. They serve as a testament to a person's values and desires for their legacy, offering clarity, protection, and peace of mind for themselves and their loved ones. However, the importance of periodic review and updating cannot be overstated, as circumstances change and evolve over time. In the subsequent chapters, we will explore additional estate planning tools and strategies to complement and enhance the effectiveness of wills, offering comprehensive guidance to navigate the complexities of estate planning with foresight and diligence.

CHAPTER 6: TRUSTS: A COMPREHENSIVE GUIDE

Trusts represent the cornerstone of sophisticated estate planning, offering individuals a robust framework to protect and manage their assets, provide for their loved ones, and achieve specific financial and philanthropic goals. In this chapter, we will embark on an in-depth exploration of trusts, delving into their multifaceted nature, intricate mechanisms, and the diverse array of benefits they offer in the realm of estate planning.

Unveiling the Intricacies of Trusts

Trusts embody a complex yet powerful legal mechanism that allows individuals to transfer assets, establish fiduciary relationships, and dictate specific instructions for the management and distribution of wealth. Understanding the nuances of trusts involves unraveling their intricate components and comprehending their various types, each tailored to serve distinct purposes and objectives within the estate planning landscape.

Types of Trusts: A Spectrum of Possibilities

1. **Revocable Living Trust**: This versatile trust allows the grantor to retain control over assets during their lifetime while facilitating seamless asset transfer upon death, bypassing the probate process. Its flexibility and privacy benefits make it a popular choice for estate planning.

2. **Irrevocable Trust**: Irrevocable trusts provide enhanced asset protection and tax advantages by permanently transferring assets out of the grantor's ownership. While relinquishing control, grantors gain valuable benefits, including creditor protection, tax minimization, and eligibility for government benefits.

3. **Testamentary Trust**: Embedded within a will, testamentary trusts spring into existence upon the grantor's death, enabling detailed asset management and distribution instructions, particularly suitable for minor children, beneficiaries with special needs, or complex family situations.

4. **Special Needs Trust**: Crafted to safeguard the financial future of individuals with disabilities, special needs trusts preserve eligibility for government benefits while enhancing quality of life through supplemental care, medical expenses, and enhanced living arrangements.

5. **Charitable Trust**: Aligned with philanthropic aspirations, charitable trusts enable individuals to leave a lasting legacy by supporting charitable causes while offering significant tax advantages and the potential for ongoing income streams for beneficiaries.

Components of a Trust: Building Blocks of Success

1. **Grantor**: The architect behind the trust, the grantor initiates the trust, transfers assets into it, and defines its parameters, reflecting their values, goals, and intentions.

2. **Trustee**: Entrusted with fiduciary duties, trustees oversee the management and administration of trust assets, acting in the best interests of beneficiaries and adhering to the trust's terms and governing law.

3. **Beneficiaries**: The ultimate recipients of trust benefits, beneficiaries stand to inherit assets, receive income

distributions, or benefit from trust provisions, as outlined by the grantor's directives.

4. **Trust Property**: The lifeblood of the trust, trust property encompasses the assets transferred into the trust, ranging from financial holdings and real estate to personal possessions and intellectual property.

5. **Trust Terms**: Captured within the trust document, trust terms delineate the rules, provisions, and conditions governing asset management, distribution, and beneficiary entitlements, ensuring clarity and adherence to the grantor's wishes.

Benefits Beyond Measure

1. **Probate Avoidance**: Trusts circumvent the probate process, expediting asset distribution, preserving privacy, and mitigating costs and delays associated with probate proceedings.

2. **Asset Protection**: Shielding assets from creditors, lawsuits, and divorces, trusts offer a robust layer of protection, safeguarding wealth for beneficiaries and future generations.

3. **Tax Efficiency**: Leveraging tax planning strategies, trusts minimize estate taxes, gift taxes, and income taxes, maximizing the value of assets passed to beneficiaries and philanthropic causes.

4. **Control and Flexibility**: Empowering grantors to dictate asset management and distribution, trusts provide unparalleled control, flexibility, and customization options to adapt to changing circumstances and priorities.

5. **Incapacity Planning**: Serving as a contingency plan, trusts ensure seamless asset management and continuity of care in the event of the grantor's incapacity, averting the need for court-appointed

guardianship or conservatorship.

Navigating the Terrain: Considerations and Best Practices

1. **Holistic Planning Approach**: Trust planning should align with overarching estate planning goals, considering factors such as family dynamics, financial objectives, and philanthropic aspirations.

2. **Selection of Trustees**: Careful selection of trustees is paramount, emphasizing competence, trustworthiness, and a commitment to fulfilling fiduciary duties with diligence and integrity.

3. **Asset Funding and Maintenance**: Proper funding and maintenance of trusts entail meticulous asset transfer, title alignment, and ongoing management to ensure the realization of trust objectives and optimize benefits.

4. **Legal and Tax Consultation**: Collaboration with legal and tax professionals is essential to navigate the complex legal landscape, ensure compliance with applicable laws, and implement tax-efficient strategies tailored to individual circumstances.

5. **Regular Review and Updates**: Trusts should undergo periodic review and updates to reflect changes in personal circumstances, family dynamics, tax laws, and regulatory environments, ensuring continued alignment with evolving objectives and priorities.

Conclusion: Embracing the Power of Trusts

In conclusion, trusts epitomize the pinnacle of estate planning sophistication, offering unparalleled benefits in asset protection, tax optimization, and legacy preservation. With a diverse array of trust types, each tailored to address specific objectives and circumstances, individuals can harness the transformative power of trusts to safeguard their wealth, provide for their loved ones, and leave a lasting impact on future generations and charitable causes. By embracing trusts as a fundamental component of their estate plans and adhering to best practices and considerations outlined in this guide, individuals can navigate the complexities of trust planning with confidence and foresight, ensuring the realization of their most cherished aspirations and legacies.

CHAPTER 7: POWERS OF ATTORNEY AND HEALTHCARE DIRECTIVES: A COMPREHENSIVE EXPLORATION

In the intricate tapestry of estate planning, Powers of Attorney (POA) and Healthcare Directives emerge as essential threads, weaving together the fabric of individual autonomy, protection, and care. Within this chapter, we embark on a profound journey into the depths of Powers of Attorney and Healthcare Directives, uncovering their profound significance, nuanced intricacies, and the transformative impact they wield in shaping the course of one's financial and medical affairs.

Unveiling the Essence of Powers of Attorney

Powers of Attorney embody a fundamental principle of agency, empowering individuals to delegate authority to trusted representatives, known as agents or attorneys-in-fact, to act on their behalf in financial and legal matters. Within the intricate tapestry of estate planning, Powers of Attorney stand as stalwart guardians, ensuring continuity and coherence in the management of assets and affairs, even in the face of incapacity or adversity.

1. **Financial Power of Attorney**: Within the realm of financial management, the Financial Power of Attorney emerges as a beacon of control and stewardship. Empowered by this instrument, agents navigate the labyrinth of financial transactions, tax matters, and asset management with vigilance and integrity, safeguarding the principal's interests and fortifying the foundations of financial security.

2. **Durable Power of Attorney**: Endowed with resilience and permanence, the Durable Power of Attorney transcends the boundaries of incapacity, standing as an unwavering sentinel of continuity and coherence. Through its enduring efficacy, individuals find solace in knowing that their financial affairs are entrusted to steadfast guardians, poised to act with unwavering fidelity in times of need.

3. **Limited or Special Power of Attorney**: In the realm of specialized transactions and finite endeavors, the Limited or Special Power of Attorney emerges as a finely honed instrument of precision and specificity. Tailored to the unique contours of particular transactions or objectives, this instrument empowers agents to navigate with precision, wielding authority with discernment and purpose.

Illuminating the Realm of Healthcare Directives

Healthcare Directives, akin to guiding stars in the constellation of medical decision-making, illuminate the path forward with clarity, compassion, and reverence for individual autonomy. Within the crucible of healthcare planning, these directives serve as beacons of empowerment, enabling individuals to articulate their values, preferences, and wishes for medical treatment and end-of-life care with grace and dignity.

1. **Living Will**: Embodied within the ethereal realm

of existential choices and profound deliberation, the Living Will transcends the boundaries of mortality, articulating the individual's preferences for medical interventions and life-sustaining treatments. Through its solemn directives, individuals find solace in knowing that their wishes will be honored with reverence and fidelity, guiding loved ones and healthcare providers with clarity and conviction.

2. **Healthcare Power of Attorney**: Within the crucible of medical decision-making, the Healthcare Power of Attorney emerges as a stalwart advocate and guardian of individual autonomy. Entrusted with the sacred duty of decision-making, healthcare proxies navigate the labyrinth of treatment options and care decisions with compassion, empathy, and unwavering fidelity to the individual's values and preferences.

Key Components: Building Blocks of Empowerment

1. **Principal**: At the heart of Powers of Attorney and Healthcare Directives lies the figure of the principal, embodying the essence of agency and autonomy. Through their deliberate actions and intentions, principals entrust authority to agents and proxies, forging a bond of trust and stewardship that transcends the boundaries of incapacity and adversity.

2. **Agent/Attorney-in-Fact**: Agents and attorneys-in-fact, the appointed custodians of authority, wield power with vigilance, integrity, and fidelity to the principal's wishes. Empowered by the mantle of responsibility, these guardians navigate the complexities of financial and medical decision-making with discernment and compassion, ensuring that the principal's interests are safeguarded with diligence and care.

3. **Healthcare Proxy/Agent**: Within the realm of healthcare decision-making, healthcare proxies stand as

compassionate stewards and advocates, empowered to navigate the labyrinth of medical treatment options and care decisions with empathy, wisdom, and reverence for the individual's values and preferences.

4. **Specific Powers and Preferences**: Powers of Attorney and Healthcare Directives, imbued with the individual's values and intentions, articulate specific powers, preferences, and instructions that guide agents and proxies in their decision-making roles. Through clear and explicit directives, principals ensure that their wishes are honored with fidelity and respect.

5. **Activation and Revocation**: These instruments, imbued with the potency of agency and autonomy, come to life through deliberate actions and intentions. Principals activate and revoke Powers of Attorney and Healthcare Directives with clarity and purpose, ensuring that their wishes are reflected with precision and fidelity.

The Profound Significance: Benefits Beyond Measure

1. **Decision-Making Authority**: Powers of Attorney and Healthcare Directives bestow individuals with the transformative power of agency, enabling them to designate trusted representatives and articulate their preferences for financial and medical decision-making with clarity and conviction.

2. **Avoidance of Guardianship Proceedings**: Through proactive planning and deliberation, individuals circumvent the pitfalls of guardianship proceedings, preserving autonomy and control over their affairs even in the face of incapacity or adversity.

3. **Clarity and Peace of Mind**: Powers of Attorney and Healthcare Directives provide clarity and guidance to loved ones and healthcare providers, alleviating uncertainty and facilitating decision-making with grace and compassion.

4. **Protection of Interests**: These instruments serve as bulwarks of protection, ensuring that individuals' financial and medical affairs are managed with integrity, dignity, and fidelity to their values and preferences.

Navigating the Terrain: Considerations and Best Practices

1. **Selection of Agents and Proxies**: Careful selection of agents and proxies is paramount, emphasizing trustworthiness, competence, and alignment with the individual's values and preferences.

2. **Communication of Wishes**: Principals should communicate their wishes and preferences regarding financial and medical matters to agents and proxies, fostering clarity, understanding, and alignment with their values and beliefs.

3. **Periodic Review and Updates**: Powers of Attorney and Healthcare Directives should undergo regular review and updates to reflect changes in circumstances, preferences, or legal requirements, ensuring continued alignment with evolving objectives and priorities.

4. **Legal and Professional Guidance**: Collaboration with legal and healthcare professionals can provide invaluable insights and guidance, ensuring compliance with applicable laws and regulations and facilitating the effective execution and implementation of Powers of Attorney and Healthcare Directives.

Conclusion: Embracing the Mantle of Empowerment

In conclusion, Powers of Attorney and Healthcare Directives stand as bastions of empowerment, embodying the transformative power of agency, autonomy, and stewardship. Through careful deliberation, proactive planning, and clear communication, individuals navigate the complexities of financial and medical decision-making with grace, integrity, and reverence for individual autonomy and dignity. In the subsequent chapters, we will explore additional facets of estate planning, offering practical guidance and insights to empower individuals on their journey toward holistic, compassionate, and purposeful planning for the future.

CHAPTER 8: GUARDIANSHIP AND CUSTODY ARRANGEMENTS: SAFEGUARDING THE FUTURE OF MINOR CHILDREN

In the intricate landscape of estate planning, few decisions carry as much weight and significance as those concerning the guardianship and custody arrangements for minor children. Rooted in the profound responsibility of ensuring the welfare and well-being of vulnerable dependents, these arrangements serve as the cornerstone of parental foresight, compassion, and love. Within this chapter, we embark on a profound exploration into the depths of guardianship and custody arrangements, illuminating their multifaceted nature, legal intricacies, and the transformative impact they hold in shaping the lives of children in times of adversity and uncertainty.

Embracing the Essence of Guardianship and Custody

Guardianship and custody arrangements embody the essence of parental stewardship and responsibility, entrusting designated individuals with the profound duty of caring for minor children in the absence of their parents. Rooted in the principles of love, protection, and foresight, these arrangements transcend legal formalities, forging bonds of trust and resilience that endure across generations.

The Legal Framework and Types of Guardianship

1. **Guardianship of the Person**: At its core, guardianship of the person encompasses the holistic care and nurturing of minor children, encompassing decisions related to education, healthcare, emotional well-being, and daily living. Guardians of the person assume the mantle of surrogate parents, providing unwavering support, guidance, and protection to children in their formative years.

2. **Guardianship of the Estate**: Beyond the realm of physical care lies the domain of financial stewardship embodied in guardianship of the estate. Guardians of the estate undertake the solemn responsibility of managing the financial affairs, assets, and inheritance of minor children, ensuring prudent management and judicious allocation of resources to secure their future.

3. **Testamentary Guardianship**: Forging a bridge between parental foresight and legal formalities, testamentary guardianship emerges as a beacon of parental empowerment and protection. Through testamentary provisions, parents nominate trusted individuals to assume guardianship of their children in the event of their incapacity or demise, imbuing their wishes with legal authority and reverence.

4. **Temporary Guardianship**: In moments of crisis and transition, temporary guardianship provides a lifeline of stability and continuity for minor children. Whether during parental illness, military deployment, or other temporary absences, temporary guardians assume the

mantle of care with compassion, resilience, and unwavering commitment to the children's well-being.

Factors to Consider When Selecting Guardians

The process of selecting guardians for minor children entails a thoughtful and introspective examination of various factors, including:

1. **Parenting Philosophy**: Aligning parenting philosophies, values, and beliefs ensures continuity and coherence in the children's upbringing, fostering a nurturing environment grounded in shared principles and ideals.

2. **Emotional Bond**: Nurturing emotional connections and bonds between children and potential guardians fosters a sense of security, trust, and belonging, laying the foundation for resilient and supportive relationships.

3. **Stability and Financial Security**: Evaluating the stability, financial security, and capacity of potential guardians ensures the provision of essential resources, opportunities, and stability essential for the children's growth and development.

4. **Parenting Skills and Capacity**: Assessing the parenting skills, capacity, and commitment of potential guardians provides assurance of their ability to meet the children's physical, emotional, and developmental needs with compassion, patience, and wisdom.

5. **Geographic Location**: Considering the geographic proximity of potential guardians facilitates continuity in the children's social, educational, and familial connections, minimizing disruptions and fostering a sense of stability and belonging.

6. **Health and Age**: Evaluating the health, age, and vitality of potential guardians ensures their ability to provide sustained care, guidance, and support throughout the children's formative years with vigor, resilience, and

unwavering dedication.

The Significance of Legal Documentation

To formalize guardianship and custody arrangements and imbue parental wishes with legal authority and reverence, parents should execute essential legal documents, including:

1. **Last Will and Testament**: Through testamentary provisions, parents nominate guardians for their minor children, articulate their wishes concerning guardianship, and ensure the continuity of care and support for their children in times of adversity and transition.

2. **Guardianship Designation Form**: In jurisdictions where available, guardianship designation forms empower parents to express their preferences for guardianship and outline specific instructions for the care and upbringing of their children in accordance with their values, beliefs, and aspirations.

3. **Custody Agreement**: In cases of divorce, separation, or co-parenting arrangements, custody agreements establish clear guidelines, roles, and responsibilities for custodial and non-custodial parents, ensuring the children's well-being and stability amidst familial transitions and dynamics.

4. **Advance Directives**: Within advance directives or healthcare proxies, parents may designate guardians for their minor children and provide instructions for medical care, treatment preferences, and decision-making on behalf of their children, ensuring their voices are heard and honored in matters of healthcare and well-being.

Legal Proceedings and Court Involvement

In instances where legal documentation is absent or contested, guardianship and custody arrangements may be subject to judicial intervention, including:

1. **Guardianship Proceedings**: In the absence of testamentary provisions or designated guardians, courts may appoint guardians for minor children based on the best interests of the children, ensuring their welfare and well-being amidst parental incapacity or demise.

2. **Custody Disputes**: Amidst divorce or parental separation, custody disputes may necessitate court intervention to determine custody arrangements, visitation schedules, and parental responsibilities, prioritizing the children's welfare and stability amidst familial transitions and dynamics.

3. **Monitoring and Oversight**: Courts may exercise ongoing monitoring and oversight of guardianship and custody arrangements, ensuring the children's best interests are upheld, guardians fulfill their duties responsibly, and the children thrive in environments of stability, love, and support.

Conclusion: Nurturing the Seeds of Resilience and Belonging

In conclusion, guardianship and custody arrangements serve as beacons of parental foresight, compassion, and love, nurturing the seeds of resilience and belonging in the hearts and minds of minor children. Through thoughtful selection, formalization through legal documentation, and adherence to the best interests of their children, parents ensure the continuity of care, stability, and well-being of their children, even in moments of adversity and uncertainty. In subsequent chapters, we will delve deeper into the multifaceted landscape of estate planning, offering comprehensive guidance and insights to empower individuals to safeguard their legacies and nurture the flourishing of future generations.

CHAPTER 9:
ESTATE TAXES: A COMPREHENSIVE EXAMINATION OF WEALTH TRANSFER DYNAMICS

Estate taxes stand as a formidable presence in the realm of wealth transfer, intricately woven into the fabric of estate planning and inheritance. Within the labyrinthine corridors of tax law and financial intricacies, the landscape of estate taxes presents a complex tapestry of exemptions, thresholds, rates, and planning strategies. In this in-depth exploration, we delve into the depths of estate taxes, unraveling their nuanced complexities, legal frameworks, planning imperatives, and profound implications for the preservation and transmission of wealth across generations.

Embracing the Essence of Estate Taxes

Estate taxes, imbued with the weight of fiscal responsibility and intergenerational wealth transfer, encapsulate the essence of financial stewardship and legacy preservation. Rooted in principles of taxation equity and revenue generation, estate taxes serve as a mechanism for governments to capture a portion of wealth accumulated over a lifetime and redistribute it for societal benefit.

The Legal Landscape and Regulatory Framework

1. **Federal Estate Tax**: The federal estate tax, governed by the Internal Revenue Service (IRS), imposes levies on the transfer of assets from a deceased individual's estate to their heirs and beneficiaries. The tax is levied based on the net value of the estate exceeding the federal exemption threshold, with rates ranging from baseline percentages to graduated tiers for larger estates.

2. **State Inheritance Taxes**: In addition to federal estate taxes, some states levy their own inheritance taxes on estate transfers, adding layers of complexity and variability to the estate planning landscape. State tax laws may feature different exemption thresholds, rates, and provisions, necessitating tailored planning strategies to optimize tax efficiency.

3. **Gift Tax and Unified Exemption**: The federal gift tax applies to lifetime transfers of assets exceeding the annual gift tax exclusion amount, with a unified exemption threshold shared with the federal estate tax. Gifts exceeding the annual exclusion amount are aggregated with the estate for tax purposes, ensuring comprehensive assessment of wealth transfers.

4. **Portability and Step-Up in Basis**: Portability provisions allow surviving spouses to inherit any unused portion of their deceased spouse's federal estate tax exemption, maximizing tax-efficient wealth transfer between spouses. Additionally, assets included in an estate receive a step-up in basis to their fair market value at the time of the decedent's death, minimizing capital gains taxes for heirs upon subsequent sale.

Strategic Tax Planning Approaches

1. **Lifetime Gifting Strategies**: Leveraging the annual gift

tax exclusion and lifetime gift tax exemption enables individuals to transfer assets to heirs during their lifetime, reducing the size of the taxable estate and potentially minimizing estate taxes. Strategic gifting plans consider factors such as timing, asset valuation, and impact on future estate tax liabilities.

2. **Irrevocable Trust Structures**: Establishing irrevocable trusts allows individuals to remove assets from their taxable estate, providing asset protection, control over distribution, and potential tax benefits. Trust structures may include grantor trusts, dynasty trusts, charitable remainder trusts, and other vehicles tailored to specific objectives and circumstances.

3. **Charitable Giving and Philanthropy**: Charitable donations and planned giving arrangements offer opportunities to reduce estate taxes while supporting charitable causes and organizations. Charitable trusts, donor-advised funds, and other philanthropic vehicles provide tax benefits, income streams, and enduring legacies of social impact.

4. **Life Insurance Planning**: Life insurance products can serve as valuable tools for estate planning, providing liquidity to pay estate taxes, equalize inheritances among heirs, or create multi-generational wealth transfer strategies. Strategies may include survivorship life insurance, irrevocable life insurance trusts (ILITs), and premium financing arrangements.

5. **Qualified Retirement Plan Optimization**: Strategic planning for qualified retirement plans, such as IRAs and 401(k)s, involves considerations of income and estate tax implications for beneficiaries. Techniques such as Roth conversions, stretch IRA strategies, and careful beneficiary designations can optimize tax efficiency and maximize wealth preservation.

Implications for Comprehensive Estate Planning

1. **Holistic Planning Approach**: Estate taxes should be integrated into a comprehensive estate planning framework that considers a range of factors, including family dynamics, financial objectives, asset protection, and charitable intentions. Coordinated planning efforts encompass wills, trusts, powers of attorney, healthcare directives, and beneficiary designations to ensure alignment with overarching objectives.

2. **Regular Review and Adjustment**: Estate plans should undergo periodic review and adjustment to reflect changes in tax laws, financial circumstances, family dynamics, and personal goals. Proactive monitoring allows for timely updates, optimizations, and adaptations to evolving regulatory environments and life circumstances.

3. **Professional Collaboration and Expertise**: Collaboration with estate planning attorneys, tax advisors, financial planners, and other professionals is essential for navigating the complexities of estate taxes and implementing effective planning strategies. Expert guidance ensures compliance with legal requirements, maximization of tax benefits, and protection of assets for future generations.

Conclusion: Navigating the Nexus of Wealth Transfer and Taxation

In conclusion, estate taxes represent a pivotal nexus where wealth transfer dynamics intersect with taxation imperatives, shaping the landscape of intergenerational wealth preservation and legacy transmission. Through a nuanced understanding of legal frameworks, strategic planning approaches, and implications for comprehensive estate planning, individuals can navigate the complexities of estate taxes with foresight, prudence, and financial acumen. In the ensuing chapters, we will delve deeper into the multifaceted terrain of estate planning, offering insights and guidance to empower individuals in their quest to preserve, protect, and perpetuate their legacies for generations to come.

CHAPTER 10: PLANNING FOR CHARITABLE GIVING: CULTIVATING ENDURING LEGACIES OF IMPACT

Charitable giving represents more than just a financial transaction; it embodies the essence of humanity's altruistic impulse to make a positive difference in the world. For individuals navigating the terrain of estate planning, philanthropy offers a profound opportunity to leave behind a legacy that extends far beyond material wealth. In this comprehensive exploration, we delve into the depths of charitable giving, illuminating its transformative power, strategic nuances, and profound implications for crafting enduring legacies of impact and social change.

Understanding the Depth of Charitable Giving

At its core, charitable giving transcends monetary donations; it encompasses the spirit of compassion, empathy, and social responsibility. Rooted in a deep-seated desire to address societal inequities, alleviate suffering, and foster human flourishing, philanthropy embodies the highest ideals of humanity's collective aspirations.

The Multi-Faceted Impact of Charitable Giving

1. **Social Transformation**: Charitable giving serves as a catalyst for social transformation, empowering marginalized communities, advancing human rights, and fostering sustainable development. By supporting organizations and initiatives addressing systemic issues such as poverty, inequality, and environmental degradation, philanthropy becomes a force for positive change on a global scale.

2. **Individual Empowerment**: Beyond its societal impact, charitable giving holds the power to transform individual lives, providing access to education, healthcare, and economic opportunities for those in need. Through scholarships, vocational training programs, and microfinance initiatives, philanthropy empowers individuals to realize their full potential and overcome barriers to success.

3. **Community Resilience**: Charitable giving strengthens the fabric of communities, fostering resilience, cohesion, and mutual support. By investing in local nonprofits, community-based organizations, and grassroots initiatives, philanthropy builds social capital, strengthens social networks, and enhances the quality of life for residents.

Strategic Approaches to Charitable Giving

1. **Values-Driven Philanthropy**: Align charitable giving with personal values, passions, and areas of interest to maximize impact and fulfillment. Whether supporting education, healthcare, environmental conservation, or arts and culture, philanthropy becomes a deeply personal expression of one's beliefs and aspirations.

2. **Strategic Grantmaking**: Adopt a strategic approach to

grantmaking, focusing on initiatives that demonstrate measurable outcomes, scalability, and sustainability. Prioritize organizations with effective leadership, sound governance structures, and a track record of impact in their respective fields.

3. **Capacity Building and Collaboration**: Invest in capacity-building initiatives and collaborative partnerships to strengthen the effectiveness and sustainability of nonprofit organizations. Support initiatives that foster collaboration, knowledge-sharing, and collective action among stakeholders to address complex social challenges.

4. **Impact Measurement and Evaluation**: Embrace rigorous impact measurement and evaluation practices to assess the effectiveness and outcomes of philanthropic investments. By tracking progress, identifying best practices, and learning from failures, philanthropists can optimize their giving strategies for greater impact over time.

Estate Planning Considerations

1. **Incorporating Charitable Intentions**: Integrate charitable intentions into estate planning documents, such as wills, trusts, and beneficiary designations. Clearly articulate legacy gifts to charitable organizations, specify the intended use of funds, and provide flexibility to adapt to changing needs and priorities.

2. **Establishing Endowed Funds**: Create endowed funds or foundations to sustain charitable giving efforts in perpetuity. Endowed funds provide a stable source of funding for charitable organizations and ensure the continuity of philanthropic legacies across generations.

3. **Donor-Advised Funds**: Consider establishing donor-advised funds (DAFs) as a flexible and tax-efficient

vehicle for charitable giving. DAFs offer donors the ability to make tax-deductible contributions, recommend grants to charitable organizations, and engage in strategic philanthropy over time.

4. **Charitable Trusts**: Explore the use of charitable remainder trusts (CRTs), charitable lead trusts (CLTs), or other planned giving vehicles to achieve philanthropic and financial objectives simultaneously. Charitable trusts offer tax advantages, income streams, and legacy planning benefits for donors and beneficiaries alike.

Cultivating a Culture of Philanthropy

1. **Family Philanthropy**: Engage family members in philanthropic activities and instill a culture of giving across generations. Involve children and grandchildren in charitable decision-making, volunteer opportunities, and experiential learning initiatives to foster a sense of social responsibility and empathy.

2. **Corporate Social Responsibility**: Extend philanthropic efforts beyond individual giving to encompass corporate social responsibility (CSR) initiatives. Align business practices with ethical principles, environmental stewardship, and community engagement to create shared value for stakeholders and society at large.

Conclusion: Shaping a Better World Through Generosity and Compassion

In conclusion, charitable giving stands as a beacon of hope, compassion, and social transformation in an increasingly complex and interconnected world. By embracing the essence of philanthropy, adopting strategic approaches to giving, and integrating charitable intentions into estate planning strategies, individuals can cultivate enduring legacies of impact that resonate across generations. As we navigate the intricacies of wealth and legacy planning, let us remember the profound words of Mahatma Gandhi: "The best way to find yourself is to lose yourself in the service of others." In the ensuing chapters, we will continue our exploration of estate planning, offering guidance and insights to empower individuals in their quest to shape a better world through generosity and compassion.

CHAPTER 11: BUSINESS SUCCESSION PLANNING: NURTURING THE CONTINUITY OF ENTREPRENEURIAL LEGACIES

Business succession planning stands as a cornerstone of estate planning, embodying the intricate balance between the preservation of entrepreneurial legacies and the seamless transition of leadership and ownership. In this chapter, we embark on an exhaustive exploration of business succession planning, delving into the depth of its strategic imperatives, legal intricacies, and practical intricacies involved in safeguarding the continuity of closely-held businesses across generations.

Embracing the Essence of Business Succession Planning

Business succession planning epitomizes the essence of forward-thinking stewardship, grounded in the conviction that the vision and values embedded within a business should transcend its founders' lifetimes. It embodies a holistic approach to safeguarding not just financial assets but also the intangible wealth of knowledge, relationships, and culture cultivated over years of entrepreneurial endeavor.

The Crucial Importance of Succession Planning

1. **Preserving Entrepreneurial Legacies**: For entrepreneurs, their business represents more than a mere source of livelihood; it is the embodiment of their dreams, aspirations, and enduring legacy. Succession planning ensures that these legacies endure, fostering continuity and perpetuating the entrepreneurial spirit across generations.

2. **Ensuring Business Continuity**: Effective succession planning is critical for ensuring the uninterrupted continuity of business operations, thereby safeguarding against disruptions and instilling confidence among stakeholders. It minimizes the risks associated with leadership transitions, enabling businesses to weather challenges and thrive in dynamic market environments.

3. **Optimizing Wealth Preservation**: Business succession planning plays a pivotal role in optimizing wealth preservation and asset protection for business owners and their families. By implementing tax-efficient strategies and structuring ownership transfers strategically, businesses can minimize tax liabilities and safeguard assets for future generations.

4. **Fostering Employee and Stakeholder Confidence**: Transparent and well-executed succession planning instills confidence among employees, customers, suppliers, and other stakeholders. It demonstrates a commitment to organizational resilience, stability, and long-term sustainability, thereby fostering trust and loyalty among key stakeholders.

Strategic Imperatives in Succession Planning

1. **Clarifying Succession Objectives**: Succession planning begins with a clear articulation of the overarching objectives and goals that the plan aims to achieve. Whether the focus is on preserving family ownership, maximizing shareholder value, or nurturing leadership continuity, clarity of purpose is paramount.

2. **Identifying and Developing Successors**: Central to succession planning is the identification and development of suitable successors who possess the requisite skills, capabilities, and values to lead the business into the future. This entails a thorough assessment of internal talent, leadership potential, and developmental needs.

3. **Selecting an Appropriate Succession Strategy**: Succession planning involves choosing the most suitable succession strategy tailored to the unique characteristics of the business, family dynamics, and owner preferences. Options may range from internal succession (promoting from within) to external succession (selling to a third party), each with its own set of advantages and challenges.

4. **Structuring Ownership Transfers**: Succession planning necessitates careful consideration of the optimal structure for transferring ownership interests, taking into account factors such as tax implications, valuation methodologies, and legal constraints. Common methods include gifting, sales, buy-sell agreements, and equity incentive plans.

5. **Addressing Legal and Regulatory Considerations**: Succession planning requires careful navigation of legal and regulatory frameworks governing business ownership transfers, including corporate governance laws, tax regulations, and industry-specific regulations. Compliance with these requirements is essential to

mitigate legal risks and ensure the validity of succession plans.

Legal and Regulatory Dimensions

1. **Structuring Entity Ownership**: Business owners must evaluate the legal structure of their enterprise and its implications for succession planning. Whether the business is structured as a sole proprietorship, partnership, corporation, or limited liability company, the choice of entity can significantly impact ownership transfers, tax treatment, and liability exposure.

2. **Drafting Comprehensive Legal Documents**: Succession planning necessitates the preparation of comprehensive legal documents to formalize ownership transfers, governance arrangements, and decision-making processes. These may include shareholder agreements, buy-sell agreements, operating agreements, employment contracts, and estate planning instruments, each tailored to address the unique needs and circumstances of the business.

3. **Compliance with Regulatory Requirements**: Business owners must ensure compliance with applicable regulatory requirements governing business ownership transfers, securities transactions, and tax reporting obligations. This may involve seeking guidance from legal counsel to navigate complex legal and regulatory frameworks and mitigate legal risks associated with succession planning.

Execution and Implementation

1. **Engaging Stakeholders and Building Consensus**: Effective succession planning entails transparent communication and engagement with key stakeholders, including family members, employees, shareholders, and advisors. Building consensus and alignment around succession objectives and strategies is essential to

garner support and minimize resistance throughout the transition process.

2. **Developing Comprehensive Succession Timelines**: Succession planning requires the establishment of clear timelines and milestones for the execution of the plan, encompassing key transition activities, ownership transfers, and leadership development initiatives. Adherence to established timelines and accountability for progress are critical to ensuring the smooth implementation of succession plans.

3. **Investing in Leadership Development and Training**: Succession planning necessitates a commitment to the development and training of potential successors to equip them with the skills, knowledge, and experience required to assume leadership roles effectively. Providing mentorship, coaching, and professional development opportunities is essential to groom future leaders and build organizational capabilities.

4. **Leveraging Professional Expertise**: Given the complexities involved in succession planning, business owners are well-advised to seek guidance from experienced advisors, including attorneys, accountants, financial planners, and business consultants. Collaborating with these professionals can help navigate legal, financial, and operational challenges, ensuring the successful implementation of succession plans.

Conclusion: Nurturing the Legacy of Entrepreneurship Across Generations

In conclusion, business succession planning represents a profound commitment to nurturing the legacy of entrepreneurship and ensuring the continuity of business enterprises across generations. By embracing the strategic imperatives, legal complexities, and practical considerations inherent in succession planning, business owners can safeguard their entrepreneurial legacies, optimize wealth preservation, and position their businesses for sustained success in the ever-evolving marketplace. In the subsequent chapters, we will continue our exploration of estate planning, offering guidance and insights to empower individuals in their quest to preserve, protect, and perpetuate their legacies across diverse dimensions of wealth and enterprise.

CHAPTER 12: PROTECTING YOUR DIGITAL ASSETS: SAFEGUARDING YOUR VIRTUAL LEGACY

In today's digital era, our lives are intricately intertwined with an expansive array of digital assets, ranging from financial accounts and intellectual property to personal memories and online identities. As individuals embark on the journey of estate planning, it becomes increasingly imperative to navigate the complexities of protecting these digital assets and preserving one's virtual legacy for future generations. In this chapter, we embark on an in-depth exploration of digital asset protection, delving into the multifaceted challenges, strategic considerations, and practical steps involved in safeguarding the integrity and accessibility of one's digital footprint.

The Ubiquity and Significance of Digital Assets

Digital assets have permeated every facet of modern life, encompassing a diverse spectrum of intangible assets stored in electronic format:

- Financial Accounts: Bank accounts, investment portfolios, cryptocurrencies.
- Intellectual Property: Copyrights, patents, trademarks,

domain names.

- Personal Data: Emails, social media profiles, digital photos and videos.
- Digital Media: E-books, music files, video content.
- Online Subscriptions: Streaming services, software licenses, membership accounts.

These digital assets hold immense value, both in terms of financial worth and sentimental significance. Failing to address digital asset protection in estate planning can lead to myriad challenges, including loss of access, security breaches, and potential legal disputes.

Understanding the Complexities of Digital Asset Protection

1. **Lack of Awareness and Understanding**: Many individuals underestimate the extent and value of their digital assets or lack a comprehensive understanding of the steps required to protect them. Without proactive planning, digital assets may be overlooked, inaccessible, or vulnerable to exploitation.

2. **Legal and Regulatory Ambiguities**: The legal and regulatory landscape surrounding digital assets is characterized by ambiguity, inconsistency, and rapid evolution. Jurisdictional complexities, disparate laws, and evolving regulations pose challenges for estate planners seeking to navigate the legal nuances of digital asset protection.

3. **Security and Privacy Risks**: Digital assets are susceptible to a myriad of security risks, including hacking attempts, data breaches, and identity theft. Safeguarding digital assets requires robust cybersecurity measures, encryption protocols, and data protection strategies to mitigate risks and safeguard sensitive information.

4. **Continuity of Access and Management**: Ensuring continuity of access to digital assets and management of online accounts after death or incapacity presents logistical challenges. Without clear instructions, designated fiduciaries, or legal frameworks in place, heirs may encounter difficulties accessing or managing digital assets on behalf of deceased individuals.

Strategic Approaches to Digital Asset Protection

1. **Comprehensive Inventory and Documentation**: Begin by creating a comprehensive inventory of all digital assets, including account credentials, passwords, and access instructions. Organize digital assets into categories and document relevant information in a secure location, such as a password-protected digital vault or encrypted storage device.

2. **Secure Password Management**: Implement secure password management practices to protect online accounts from unauthorized access. Utilize reputable password managers to generate strong, unique passwords for each account and enable multi-factor authentication where available to enhance security.

3. **Integration with Estate Planning Documents**: Incorporate provisions for digital asset protection into estate planning documents, such as wills, trusts, and powers of attorney. Specify instructions for accessing and transferring digital assets, designate digital executors or trustees, and outline preferences for the disposition of digital assets in accordance with your wishes.

4. **Utilization of Digital Estate Planning Services**: Consider leveraging digital estate planning services and platforms that specialize in managing and transferring digital assets. These services offer secure storage, encryption, and access controls for digital assets,

facilitating seamless transfer and management upon death or incapacity.

Legal and Regulatory Considerations

1. **Compliance with Terms of Service Agreements**: Review and understand the terms of service agreements governing online accounts and digital platforms. Some platforms have specific provisions regarding the transfer or management of digital assets upon death, which may impact estate planning strategies.

2. **Authorization and Consent Mechanisms**: Obtain explicit authorization and consent from account holders for the management or transfer of digital assets, where applicable. Certain jurisdictions have enacted laws granting fiduciaries legal authority to access and manage digital assets on behalf of deceased individuals, subject to compliance with legal requirements and privacy considerations.

3. **Designation of Digital Executors or Trustees**: Consider designating a digital executor or trustee with specialized knowledge and expertise in managing digital assets. This individual can oversee the administration of digital assets, coordinate with service providers, and ensure compliance with legal and regulatory requirements governing digital asset protection.

Conclusion: Navigating the Digital Frontier of Estate Planning

In conclusion, protecting your digital assets is an essential component of modern estate planning, requiring proactive strategies, careful consideration, and ongoing vigilance. By understanding the complexities, implementing strategic measures, and addressing legal and regulatory considerations, individuals can safeguard their digital footprint and preserve their virtual legacy for future generations. As we navigate the digital frontier of estate planning, let us remain cognizant of the evolving nature of digital assets and the importance of adapting our strategies to protect and preserve our digital legacies in an ever-changing digital landscape.

CHAPTER 13: ESTATE PLANNING FOR BLENDED FAMILIES: NAVIGATING COMPLEX DYNAMICS AND ENSURING FAIRNESS

Estate planning for blended families demands a profound understanding of intricate family dynamics, financial complexities, and emotional sensitivities. Blended families, often comprising individuals who have remarried or formed new partnerships after previous relationships, present unique challenges that require careful navigation and strategic planning. In this chapter, we delve deeply into the multifaceted considerations, nuanced approaches, and practical strategies involved in crafting estate plans that accommodate the diverse needs, aspirations, and relationships within blended families while upholding principles of fairness, equity, and unity across generations.

Embracing the Complexity of Blended Families

Blended families embody a tapestry of relationships, histories, and identities, characterized by diverse family structures and dynamics:

- Stepchildren: Children from previous relationships of one or both partners, who may have varying degrees of emotional and financial attachment to the blended family.

- Blended Siblings: Children born to the current relationship, shared between both partners, who may navigate complex dynamics with their step-siblings.

- Ex-Spouses: Former spouses or partners who may retain legal or financial ties, impacting estate planning considerations such as alimony, child support, and property division.

- Extended Family: Additional relatives, such as grandparents, aunts, uncles, and cousins, who may play significant roles in the blended family dynamic and inheritance considerations.

Each member of a blended family brings their own unique perspectives, needs, and expectations to the estate planning process, necessitating a holistic and inclusive approach that acknowledges and respects the complexity of familial relationships.

Navigating the Financial Landscape

1. **Addressing Financial Obligations**: Take stock of financial obligations to former spouses or children from previous relationships, including alimony, child support, and educational expenses. Ensure that these obligations are factored into estate planning documents and adequately addressed to prevent disputes or legal challenges that could disrupt family harmony.

2. **Balancing Financial Resources**: Strive to achieve a delicate balance between meeting the financial needs of current and previous family members while maintaining fairness and equity in the distribution of

assets. Tailor estate plans to accommodate individual circumstances, provide for dependents, and promote harmony among blended family members.

3. **Protecting Vulnerable Beneficiaries**: Identify and protect vulnerable beneficiaries within the blended family, such as minor children, elderly parents, or individuals with special needs, through appropriate estate planning mechanisms. Establish trusts, guardianships, or conservatorships to ensure their welfare and financial security, taking into account their unique needs and circumstances.

Promoting Unity and Fairness

1. **Fostering Open Communication**: Cultivate an environment of open communication and transparency among all members of the blended family, encouraging honest dialogue about financial matters, inheritance expectations, and estate planning preferences. Facilitate discussions to address concerns, clarify intentions, and promote understanding among family members.

2. **Balancing Needs and Fairness**: Strive to achieve a balance between meeting the individual needs of family members and upholding principles of fairness and equity in estate planning decisions. Consider factors such as financial contributions, caregiving responsibilities, and emotional bonds when determining asset distribution and inheritance provisions.

3. **Mediating Conflicts and Disputes**: Anticipate potential sources of conflict or disputes within the blended family and proactively implement strategies to minimize tensions. Engage the services of a qualified mediator or family therapist to facilitate constructive dialogue, resolve conflicts, and foster reconciliation among family members.

Strategic Approaches to Estate Planning

1. **Customized Estate Planning Documents**: Develop customized estate planning documents, including wills, trusts, powers of attorney, and healthcare directives, that reflect the unique needs and circumstances of the blended family. Tailor provisions to address individual preferences, family dynamics, and asset distribution goals, ensuring clarity and specificity in all directives.

2. **Trust-Based Planning Strategies**: Utilize trusts as central components of estate plans for blended families to achieve flexibility, control, and asset protection objectives. Establish trusts to provide for surviving spouses, children from previous relationships, and blended siblings, ensuring that each beneficiary's needs are met while preserving family harmony and unity.

3. **Pre- and Postnuptial Agreements**: Consider prenuptial or postnuptial agreements to delineate financial rights, obligations, and expectations between spouses in blended families. These agreements can clarify property ownership, inheritance rights, and estate distribution preferences, reducing ambiguity and potential disputes in the event of divorce or death.

4. **Beneficiary Designations and Titling**: Review and update beneficiary designations on retirement accounts, life insurance policies, and other financial assets to reflect current family dynamics and preferences. Ensure that assets are titled appropriately to align with estate planning goals and minimize probate and tax implications, taking into account considerations such as survivorship rights and contingent beneficiaries.

Legal and Regulatory Considerations

1. **Legal Recognition of Blended Relationships**: Be mindful of legal recognition of blended relationships,

including marriage, domestic partnership, and cohabitation, which may vary depending on jurisdiction. Understand the legal rights and obligations conferred by these relationships and their implications for estate planning, including spousal rights of inheritance, property rights, and intestacy laws.

2. **Inheritance Laws and Intestacy Rules**: Familiarize yourself with inheritance laws and intestacy rules governing blended families in your jurisdiction. In the absence of valid estate planning documents, these laws dictate the distribution of assets among surviving family members, which may not align with your wishes or family dynamics. Consult with an experienced estate planning attorney to ensure compliance with legal requirements and optimize asset distribution outcomes for your blended family.

3. **Estate Tax Planning Strategies**: Consider estate tax implications for blended families, including spousal exemptions, gift tax exclusions, and generation-skipping transfer tax considerations. Work closely with tax professionals and estate planning attorneys to develop tax-efficient strategies that maximize wealth preservation and minimize tax liabilities for all family members, taking into account factors such as asset titling, trust structures, and charitable giving.

Conclusion: Cultivating Harmony and Legacy Preservation in Blended Families

In conclusion, estate planning for blended families requires a comprehensive and nuanced approach that acknowledges the complexity of familial relationships, financial obligations, and emotional dynamics. By embracing open communication, fostering unity, and implementing strategic planning strategies, individuals can navigate the intricacies of blended family estate planning with confidence and clarity, ensuring that their legacy endures and flourishes for the benefit of all family members. As we embark on the journey of estate planning, let us remain committed to promoting harmony, understanding, and legacy preservation within our blended families, fostering a legacy of unity, love, and prosperity across generations.

CHAPTER 14: SPECIAL CONSIDERATIONS FOR ELDERLY INDIVIDUALS: TAILORING ESTATE PLANNING TO LIFE'S LATER CHAPTERS

As individuals transition into their later years, estate planning takes on added significance, serving as a critical tool for ensuring personal well-being, preserving financial resources, and shaping lasting legacies. In this chapter, we delve into the nuanced considerations, complex challenges, and strategic approaches involved in estate planning for elderly individuals. By embracing the unique circumstances, health-related concerns, and legacy preservation goals of later-life planning, elderly individuals can navigate life's later chapters with confidence, dignity, and peace of mind.

Acknowledging the Significance of Later-Life Estate Planning

1. **Navigating Evolving Needs**: As individuals age, their priorities, preferences, and needs evolve, necessitating a comprehensive reassessment of estate planning goals and strategies. Later-life estate planning provides an opportunity to address changing circumstances,

anticipate future challenges, and make provisions for healthcare, long-term care, and end-of-life preferences.

2. **Ensuring Personal Well-being**: Estate planning for elderly individuals extends beyond financial considerations to encompass personal well-being, healthcare preferences, and quality of life. By proactively addressing medical directives, powers of attorney, and advance care planning, individuals can assert control over their healthcare decisions and ensure that their wishes are honored in the event of incapacity or terminal illness.

Health-Related Considerations

1. **Advance Healthcare Directives**: Drafting advance healthcare directives, such as living wills and healthcare proxies, empowers elderly individuals to specify their medical preferences, treatment preferences, and end-of-life care wishes. These documents serve as invaluable tools for guiding healthcare decisions and ensuring that individuals receive care aligned with their values and preferences.

2. **Long-Term Care Planning**: Anticipating the potential need for long-term care services is essential for elderly individuals. Long-term care planning involves evaluating care options, assessing financial resources, and implementing strategies to fund long-term care expenses, such as long-term care insurance, Medicaid planning, or asset protection trusts. By proactively planning for long-term care needs, individuals can secure access to quality care while protecting their financial security and preserving assets for future generations.

Financial and Legal Considerations

1. **Asset Protection Strategies**: Safeguarding assets from the high costs of long-term care and medical expenses

is a priority for elderly individuals. Asset protection strategies, such as irrevocable trusts, gifting, and annuities, can help shield assets while preserving eligibility for government benefits, such as Medicaid or veterans' benefits, to cover long-term care costs. By implementing asset protection strategies, individuals can mitigate the financial risks associated with aging and ensure that their assets are preserved for their own use and for the benefit of their loved ones.

2. **Estate Tax Planning**: Reviewing estate tax implications and implementing tax-efficient strategies is crucial for elderly individuals with substantial assets. By maximizing available tax exemptions, utilizing charitable giving strategies, and structuring estate plans to minimize tax liabilities, individuals can preserve wealth for future generations and minimize tax burdens on their estates. Estate tax planning also involves considering the impact of estate tax laws and regulations on estate distribution and ensuring that estate plans are structured to optimize tax savings while achieving individuals' legacy preservation goals.

Legacy and End-of-Life Planning

1. **Legacy Preservation Goals**: Articulating legacy preservation goals and intentions allows elderly individuals to shape their lasting impact on future generations. Whether through charitable giving, family heirlooms, or personal legacies, individuals can leave behind a meaningful and enduring legacy that reflects their values, passions, and life experiences. Legacy planning involves identifying meaningful ways to leave a positive and lasting impact on the world and ensuring that individuals' values and beliefs are passed down to future generations.

2. **Funeral and Burial Preferences**: Documenting funeral

and burial preferences ensures that individuals' wishes are respected and honored after their passing. By specifying burial arrangements, memorial services, and funeral expenses in advance, elderly individuals can alleviate the burden on loved ones and ensure that their final wishes are carried out with dignity and respect. Funeral and burial planning also involves considering cultural and religious traditions, personal preferences, and family dynamics to ensure that individuals' final wishes are fulfilled in a manner that reflects their values and beliefs.

Family Dynamics and Interpersonal Considerations

1. **Family Communication and Inclusion**: Engaging in open and honest communication with family members about estate planning intentions, healthcare preferences, and end-of-life wishes fosters understanding, transparency, and unity within the family. Involving family members in the estate planning process can mitigate misunderstandings, prevent disputes, and promote harmony among loved ones. By fostering open communication and inclusion, elderly individuals can ensure that their wishes are understood and respected by their loved ones and that family relationships are strengthened through the estate planning process.

2. **Appointment of Trusted Representatives**: Selecting trusted representatives, such as healthcare proxies, powers of attorney, and executors, is critical for elderly individuals. These individuals should be chosen based on their competence, reliability, and alignment with the individual's values and preferences, ensuring that important decisions are made in their best interests. By appointing trusted representatives, individuals can ensure that their wishes are carried out and that their interests are protected during times of incapacity or

after their passing.

Conclusion: Empowering Elderly Individuals to Navigate Life's Later Chapters with Confidence and Peace of Mind

In conclusion, estate planning for elderly individuals is a multifaceted and deeply personal process that requires careful consideration of health-related concerns, financial considerations, legacy preservation goals, and family dynamics. By embracing the significance of later-life estate planning and proactively addressing these considerations, elderly individuals can navigate life's later chapters with confidence, dignity, and peace of mind. As we embark on the journey of later-life estate planning, let us remain committed to empowering elderly individuals to assert control over their futures, honor their legacies, and provide for their loved ones with grace, dignity, and compassion.

CHAPTER 15: PLANNING FOR PERSONS WITH SPECIAL NEEDS: ENSURING FINANCIAL SECURITY, CARE, AND QUALITY OF LIFE

Estate planning for individuals with special needs encompasses a comprehensive approach that addresses not only financial considerations but also healthcare, housing, employment, and legal protections. Understanding the intricacies of planning for persons with special needs requires a deeper exploration of the challenges they face, the resources available to support them, and the strategies that can help safeguard their well-being and quality of life. In this chapter, we delve into the multifaceted aspects of planning for persons with special needs, offering insights and guidance to empower families and caregivers in navigating this complex terrain.

Understanding the Needs of Persons with Special Needs

1. **Diverse Range of Special Needs**: Persons with special needs encompass a wide spectrum of disabilities, each

with its own unique characteristics, challenges, and requirements. From physical disabilities and cognitive impairments to developmental disorders and sensory sensitivities, understanding the specific needs and abilities of individuals is crucial for developing tailored estate planning strategies.

2. **Lifetime Support Considerations**: Unlike typical estate planning, which often focuses on transferring assets to beneficiaries upon death, planning for persons with special needs requires a lifelong perspective. Individuals with special needs may require ongoing support and assistance throughout their lives, necessitating careful consideration of long-term care, financial management, and guardianship arrangements.

Preserving Eligibility for Government Benefits

1. **Special Needs Trusts (SNTs)**: Special Needs Trusts (SNTs) serve as a cornerstone of estate planning for persons with special needs, allowing families to provide supplemental financial support without jeopardizing eligibility for means-tested government benefits. Establishing an SNT enables individuals to receive assistance for expenses not covered by public benefits, such as medical treatments, therapies, housing, transportation, and recreational activities.

2. **Understanding SNT Administration**: Effective administration of an SNT requires careful attention to compliance with complex rules and regulations governing benefit eligibility. Trustees must navigate restrictions on distributions, reporting requirements, and fiduciary responsibilities to ensure that trust funds are used in a manner that maximizes the beneficiary's quality of life while preserving essential benefits.

Providing Supplemental Care and Support

1. **Care Coordination and Advocacy**: Coordinating

care and advocating for individuals with special needs involves collaborating with a diverse array of professionals, including healthcare providers, educators, social workers, and disability advocates. Care coordinators can help families navigate the complexities of the healthcare system, access community resources, and develop individualized care plans that address the unique needs and preferences of the individual.

2. **Holistic Support Services**: Beyond financial assistance, individuals with special needs may require a range of support services to enhance their overall well-being and quality of life. These services may include assistive technology, adaptive equipment, therapeutic interventions, vocational training, behavioral support, and social skills development programs tailored to the individual's strengths and challenges.

Ensuring a High Quality of Life

1. **Housing and Residential Options**: Securing appropriate housing accommodations is a fundamental aspect of planning for persons with special needs. Depending on the individual's level of independence and support needs, housing options may range from independent living arrangements with supportive services to group homes or residential facilities staffed by trained professionals.

2. **Employment and Community Integration**: Promoting opportunities for employment, vocational training, and community integration is essential for enhancing the independence, self-esteem, and social inclusion of individuals with special needs. Supported employment programs, job coaching services, and community-based activities can empower individuals to contribute to society, develop meaningful relationships, and pursue

their personal goals and interests.

Legal and Regulatory Considerations

1. **Guardianship and Alternatives**: Determining the need for guardianship or conservatorship involves assessing the individual's capacity to make decisions and manage their affairs independently. While guardianship may be necessary for individuals who lack the capacity to make informed decisions, alternatives such as supported decision-making agreements or limited guardianship arrangements should be explored to maximize autonomy and self-determination.

2. **Special Education Rights**: Understanding the rights and protections afforded to individuals with special needs under federal and state special education laws is essential for advocating for appropriate educational services and accommodations. Families should familiarize themselves with Individualized Education Programs (IEPs), Section 504 Plans, and other legal mechanisms designed to ensure access to a free and appropriate public education for individuals with disabilities.

Conclusion: Empowering Persons with Special Needs and Their Families

In conclusion, estate planning for persons with special needs requires a holistic and individualized approach that addresses their unique circumstances, challenges, and aspirations. By preserving eligibility for government benefits, providing supplemental care and support, and promoting opportunities for independence and inclusion, families can empower individuals with special needs to lead fulfilling and meaningful lives. As we navigate the complexities of planning for persons with special needs, let us remain committed to promoting dignity, equality, and opportunity for all individuals, regardless of ability or disability.

CHAPTER 16: ESTATE PLANNING FOR INTERNATIONAL ASSETS: NAVIGATING COMPLEXITIES ACROSS BORDERS

In an era of globalization, individuals often find themselves with assets spread across multiple countries, whether due to business ventures, investment opportunities, or personal circumstances. Estate planning for international assets involves navigating a complex web of legal, tax, and cultural considerations that can significantly impact the transfer, protection, and distribution of wealth across borders. In this chapter, we delve deeper into the intricacies of international estate planning, exploring the nuances of cross-border taxation, legal structures, succession planning, compliance obligations, and strategies for optimizing wealth preservation.

Understanding the Scope and Diversity of International Assets

1. **Multifaceted Nature of International Assets**: International assets encompass a diverse array of holdings, including real estate properties, financial accounts, investment portfolios, business interests,

intellectual property rights, and personal belongings located in different jurisdictions. Each type of asset presents unique challenges and opportunities for estate planning, requiring a nuanced understanding of local laws, regulations, and cultural norms.

2. **Global Mobility and Diversification**: Individuals may acquire international assets for various reasons, such as business expansion, investment diversification, lifestyle preferences, or family connections. Diversifying assets across different countries can offer benefits such as risk mitigation, currency diversification, access to global markets, and opportunities for capital appreciation, but it also introduces complexities in managing and transferring wealth across borders.

Cross-Border Taxation Considerations

1. **Residency, Domicile, and Tax Status**: Determining an individual's tax residency, domicile status, and tax obligations in multiple jurisdictions is a fundamental aspect of international estate planning. Tax residency rules vary by country and may depend on factors such as physical presence, immigration status, and economic ties. Dual residency or domicile can lead to overlapping tax liabilities and compliance obligations, requiring careful planning to mitigate potential tax consequences.

2. **Double Taxation Relief and Tax Treaties**: Tax treaties between countries often contain provisions for relieving double taxation on income, capital gains, and inheritances. Understanding the provisions of relevant tax treaties and leveraging available relief mechanisms can help individuals minimize tax liabilities and optimize tax efficiency when transferring assets across borders. However, navigating the complexities of tax treaties requires expert guidance to ensure compliance and maximize tax savings.

Legal Structures and Estate Planning Strategies

1. **International Wills and Testamentary Documents**: Drafting international wills and testamentary documents is essential for ensuring that assets located in different jurisdictions are distributed according to the individual's wishes. International wills may include provisions addressing the validity of the document across borders, choice of law clauses, and appointment of executors or personal representatives with international expertise. However, the recognition and enforcement of international wills can vary by jurisdiction, highlighting the importance of seeking legal advice to ensure compliance with local laws.

2. **Trusts and Offshore Structures**: Trusts and offshore structures can offer valuable benefits for international estate planning, including asset protection, tax efficiency, privacy, and flexibility in wealth transfer. Offshore trusts, foundations, and corporations may be used to hold international assets, shield assets from creditors or legal claims, and facilitate the transfer of wealth to future generations. However, structuring offshore entities requires careful consideration of regulatory requirements, tax implications, and compliance obligations in both the home and host jurisdictions.

Succession Planning and Asset Distribution

1. **Forced Heirship and Inheritance Laws**: Inheritance laws and forced heirship rules vary widely from country to country and can significantly impact the distribution of assets located within the jurisdiction. Forced heirship regimes may impose mandatory inheritance shares for certain family members, restrict testamentary freedom, or require specific formalities for will execution. Understanding the implications of forced heirship laws

and planning accordingly is essential for preserving individuals' testamentary wishes and avoiding disputes among heirs.

2. **Coordination of Estate Plans Across Jurisdictions**: Coordinating estate plans across multiple jurisdictions is critical for avoiding conflicts of law, duplicative probate proceedings, and unintended consequences in asset distribution. This may involve aligning wills, trusts, and other testamentary documents with local legal requirements, appointing executors or trustees with international expertise, and implementing mechanisms for seamless transfer of assets across borders. Collaborating with legal and tax advisors who specialize in international estate planning can help individuals develop integrated estate plans that address the complexities of cross-border asset ownership.

Compliance and Reporting Obligations

1. **Foreign Account Reporting Requirements**: Individuals with international assets may be subject to various reporting obligations, including Foreign Bank Account Reports (FBAR), Foreign Account Tax Compliance Act (FATCA) reporting, and disclosures of foreign financial assets on tax returns. Failing to comply with reporting requirements can result in severe penalties, fines, and legal consequences. Staying abreast of changing regulatory requirements and maintaining accurate records of international financial transactions is essential for avoiding compliance pitfalls and minimizing regulatory risks.

2. **Estate and Inheritance Tax Filings**: Estate and inheritance tax filings may be required in multiple jurisdictions where assets are located or where beneficiaries reside. Understanding the filing requirements, deadlines, and tax implications of estate

transfers is essential for minimizing tax liabilities and ensuring compliance with local tax authorities. This may involve engaging tax professionals with expertise in international taxation to navigate complex tax laws, optimize tax planning strategies, and mitigate potential tax exposures.

Conclusion: Strategic Planning for Global Wealth Management

In conclusion, estate planning for international assets demands a strategic and proactive approach that addresses the complexities of cross-border taxation, legal structures, succession planning, and compliance obligations. By understanding the implications of owning assets abroad, leveraging available tax treaties and relief mechanisms, and coordinating estate plans across jurisdictions, individuals can safeguard their wealth, minimize tax liabilities, and ensure a seamless transfer of assets to future generations. As we navigate the intricacies of international estate planning, let us remain committed to optimizing wealth preservation, protecting assets, and facilitating the efficient transfer of wealth across borders in accordance with individuals' wishes and aspirations.

CHAPTER 17: HANDLING PROBATE AND ADMINISTRATION: NAVIGATING THE LEGAL PROCESS OF ESTATE SETTLEMENT

Probate and estate administration are pivotal stages in the transfer of assets and settlement of an individual's estate following their demise. This chapter delves into the intricate aspects of probate and estate administration, offering a comprehensive exploration of the legal processes, roles of executors or administrators, potential obstacles, and strategies for efficient estate settlement. By delving deeper into the probate process and adopting effective administration techniques, individuals can ensure the orderly distribution of assets, fulfill their fiduciary duties, and minimize conflicts among beneficiaries.

The Essence of Probate and Estate Administration

1. **Comprehending Probate's Essence**: Probate stands as the legal avenue through which the assets of a deceased

individual are disbursed and their debts settled under the watchful eye of the court. Its primary purpose is to oversee the orderly transfer of assets, be it in compliance with the terms of the will or the legalities of intestacy in the absence of a will. This process further serves to resolve disputes, authenticate the validity of the will, and appoint executors or administrators to supervise the estate's liquidation.

2. **Roles and Duties**: Executors, also known as personal representatives, play a pivotal role in executing the wishes of the deceased as articulated in the will or as mandated by intestacy laws. Their obligations include identifying and cataloging assets, clearing debts and taxes, disseminating assets to beneficiaries, and filing requisite court documentation. These executors must adhere strictly to fiduciary standards, exhibiting care, loyalty, and impartiality in managing estate assets for the beneficiaries' benefit.

Commencing the Probate Process

1. **Inaugurating with Petition Filing**: Probate procedures generally commence with the filing of a petition or application with the probate court in the jurisdiction where the deceased resided. This petition usually aims to validate the will, designate an executor or administrator, and inaugurate formal estate proceedings. In instances where the deceased has passed without a will, the court appoints an administrator to steer the estate settlement.

2. **Disseminating Notice**: Executors or administrators shoulder the responsibility of disseminating notice of the probate proceedings to pertinent parties. Interested parties include named beneficiaries, intestate heirs, creditors, and other concerned individuals. Notices are disseminated through legal publications, direct

mailings, or electronic notifications in adherence to local court protocols.

Asset Inventorying and Debt Resolution

1. **Asset Identification and Valuation**: Executors undertake the arduous task of identifying, locating, and assessing the value of all assets owned by the deceased at the time of their demise. This entails an exhaustive search for real estate, financial holdings, personal effects, business interests, and other assets subject to probate. Professional appraisals and financial assessments aid in determining the fair market value, crucial for estate administration.

2. **Debt Clearance and Creditor Claims**: Executors bear the responsibility of identifying and settling legitimate debts of the estate, encompassing funeral costs, outstanding liabilities, taxes, and administrative expenses. Creditors must be apprised of the deceased's demise and given an opportunity to assert their claims within a stipulated timeframe. Executors are tasked with scrutinizing and adjudicating these claims, disputing invalid assertions, and ensuring the orderly settlement of debts in conformity with statutory hierarchies.

Asset Dissemination to Beneficiaries

1. **Estate Liquidation and Allocation**: Following debt resolution and expense settlement, executors embark on disbursing remaining assets to beneficiaries in line with the will's dictates or the laws of intestacy. Asset distribution might necessitate the transfer of ownership, liquidation of holdings, sale of property, or establishment of trusts for underage or incapacitated beneficiaries. Executors must secure court endorsement for distribution plans and compile final accounts detailing all estate transactions.

2. **Finalizing Probate Proceedings**: Once assets have been disseminated, and estate affairs resolved, executors petition the probate court for final approval. This entails filing conclusive reports and accounts, seeking judicial concurrence for estate closure. Upon the court's approval of the final settlement and distribution, the estate administration draws to a close, and executors are relieved of their duties.

Challenges and Conflict Resolution

1. **Contesting Wills and Disputes**: Probate proceedings may be marred by contentious disputes and challenges from aggrieved heirs, beneficiaries, or creditors. Allegations of fraud, coercion, incapacity, or other grounds may be advanced to invalidate the will or impugn estate administration. Executors must navigate these disputes meticulously, upholding transparency, adhering to legal protocols, and protecting the integrity of the estate settlement process.

2. **Mediation and Litigation**: Resolution of disputes during probate proceedings may necessitate resorting to alternative dispute resolution mechanisms like mediation or arbitration to preclude protracted litigation. Mediation offers a forum for parties to negotiate and achieve mutually acceptable resolutions under the guidance of an impartial mediator. Should amicable resolutions prove elusive, litigation becomes inevitable, wherein judicial intervention is sought to adjudicate contested matters and provide legal clarifications.

Strategies for Streamlined Estate Settlement

1. **Meticulous Planning and Documentation**: Astute estate planning and comprehensive documentation pave the way for streamlined probate procedures and efficient estate settlement. Individuals should maintain

updated wills, trusts, beneficiary designations, and other estate planning instruments to ensure clarity, enforceability, and adherence to testamentary wishes.

2. **Transparent Communication and Collaboration**: Executors ought to foster transparent communication with beneficiaries, creditors, and other stakeholders throughout the probate process to obviate misunderstandings and address concerns promptly. Collaborating with legal, financial, and tax advisors can furnish invaluable guidance and expertise in navigating intricate legal and financial issues encountered during estate administration.

Conclusion: Preserving the Integrity of Estate Settlement

In conclusion, navigating probate and estate administration demands meticulous adherence to legal protocols, fiduciary obligations, and open communication to ensure the seamless distribution of assets. By acquainting themselves with the probate process, discharging fiduciary responsibilities, and implementing efficient administration strategies, executors can navigate complexities, mitigate conflicts, and expedite the transfer of wealth to beneficiaries. As stewards of the decedent's legacy, executors occupy a pivotal role in preserving assets, honoring testamentary directives, and fostering equitable wealth distribution in accordance with legal precepts.

CHAPTER 18: REVIEWING AND UPDATING YOUR ESTATE PLAN REGULARLY: ENSURING ALIGNMENT WITH EVOLVING CIRCUMSTANCES

Estate planning is a dynamic process that requires continual evaluation and adjustment to remain effective in fulfilling your objectives. In this chapter, we delve deeply into the critical importance of regularly reviewing and updating your estate plan. We explore the multifaceted nature of estate planning, the intricacies involved in periodic reviews, and the strategies for ensuring that your plan remains aligned with your evolving circumstances and goals. By embracing a proactive approach to estate planning maintenance, individuals can protect their assets, preserve their legacy, and provide for their loved ones with confidence and clarity.

Understanding the Dynamics of Estate Planning

1. **Holistic Approach**: Estate planning encompasses more than just the distribution of assets upon death. It involves a comprehensive assessment of your financial situation, family dynamics, personal values, and long-term goals. By considering all these factors, you can create a plan that addresses your unique needs and priorities.

2. **Interconnected Components**: An estate plan consists of various interrelated components, including wills, trusts, powers of attorney, healthcare directives, and beneficiary designations. Changes to any of these elements can have far-reaching implications for the overall effectiveness of your plan.

The Importance of Regular Review and Updates

1. **Adapting to Life Changes**: Life is fluid, marked by transitions and milestones that can impact your estate planning needs. Events such as marriage, divorce, birth of children, changes in health, career advancements, or relocation may necessitate revisions to your plan to reflect your current circumstances and intentions.

2. **Maintaining Relevance**: Laws and regulations governing estate planning are subject to change, as are tax laws, healthcare policies, and family dynamics. Regular reviews ensure that your plan remains up-to-date and compliant with current legal requirements, minimizing the risk of unintended consequences or disputes.

Key Areas for Review and Update

1. **Legal Documents**: Begin by reviewing your will, trust agreements, and other legal documents to ensure they accurately reflect your wishes. Pay close attention

to beneficiary designations, trustee appointments, and distribution provisions to verify their alignment with your current preferences.

2. **Asset Ownership and Titling**: Review the ownership and titling of your assets to ensure they align with your estate planning goals. Consider whether changes in ownership structures, such as transferring assets to a trust or establishing joint tenancy, may be beneficial for asset protection or distribution purposes.

3. **Beneficiary Designations**: Evaluate beneficiary designations on retirement accounts, life insurance policies, and investment accounts to confirm they reflect your current wishes. Changes in family circumstances or relationships may necessitate updates to ensure assets pass to the intended beneficiaries.

4. **Fiduciary Appointments**: Assess the individuals named as executors, trustees, guardians, or agents in your estate planning documents. Confirm their willingness and ability to fulfill their roles effectively, and consider whether changes in relationships or circumstances warrant appointing alternate fiduciaries.

Triggers for Estate Plan Updates

1. **Life Events**: Major life events such as marriage, divorce, birth or adoption of children, or the death of a spouse or beneficiary often trigger the need for estate plan updates. These events can alter your family structure, financial obligations, and priorities, necessitating corresponding adjustments to your plan.

2. **Financial Changes**: Significant changes in your financial situation, such as inheritance, business transactions, investment gains or losses, or changes in income or expenses, may require revisions to your estate plan. Ensure that your plan reflects your current assets, liabilities, and wealth distribution goals.

3. **Health Considerations**: Changes in health status, such as diagnosis of a serious illness, disability, or decline in cognitive function, may necessitate updates to your healthcare directives and powers of attorney. Review your preferences for medical treatment, end-of-life care, and decision-making authority to ensure they align with your current wishes.

4. **Legal and Tax Updates**: Stay informed about changes in laws and regulations governing estate planning, taxation, and healthcare directives. Consult with legal and tax professionals to assess the impact of these changes on your estate plan and identify opportunities for optimization or mitigation.

Strategies for Effective Maintenance

1. **Scheduled Reviews**: Establish a regular schedule for reviewing your estate plan, such as annually or biennially, to coincide with significant life events or changes in tax laws. Use these reviews as opportunities to assess your goals, update your documents, and consult with professionals as needed.

2. **Professional Guidance**: Work with experienced estate planning attorneys, financial advisors, and tax professionals to guide you through the review and update process. These professionals can provide valuable insights, identify potential issues, and offer tailored solutions to address your specific needs and objectives.

3. **Open Communication**: Communicate changes in your estate plan to relevant parties, including family members, fiduciaries, and financial institutions. Ensure that updated documents are properly executed, distributed, and stored in a secure location accessible to trusted individuals.

4. **Stay Informed**: Stay abreast of changes in laws,

regulations, and estate planning strategies that may impact your plan. Attend seminars, workshops, or webinars, and subscribe to newsletters or publications from reputable sources to stay informed about relevant developments in the field.

Conclusion: Embracing Proactive Maintenance for Peace of Mind

In conclusion, regular review and updating of your estate plan are essential components of effective estate planning. By embracing a proactive approach to maintenance and remaining vigilant to changes in your life circumstances and the legal landscape, you can ensure that your plan remains relevant, compliant, and aligned with your evolving goals and priorities. By investing time and effort into the ongoing care of your estate plan, you can achieve peace of mind knowing that your wishes will be honored, your assets protected, and your legacy preserved for generations to come.

CHAPTER 19: WILL PLANNING CHECKLIST

Preparing for Will Planning

1. **Gather Information**: Compile a list of your assets, liabilities, and important documents, including bank accounts, investment accounts, real estate holdings, retirement accounts, insurance policies, and debts.

2. **Identify Beneficiaries**: Determine who you want to inherit your assets and how you want them to be distributed. Consider family members, friends, charitable organizations, and other beneficiaries.

3. **Select Executors**: Choose one or more trusted individuals to serve as executors of your will. Executors are responsible for managing your estate, paying debts and taxes, and distributing assets to beneficiaries.

Creating Your Will

4. **Consult with Legal Professionals**: Seek guidance from an experienced estate planning attorney to ensure your will complies with state laws and accurately reflects your wishes. Legal professionals can provide valuable advice and draft your will to address your specific needs.

5. **Draft Your Will**: Work with your attorney to draft your will, including provisions for asset distribution, appointment of executors and guardians, and any specific instructions or wishes you have regarding your estate.

6. **Review and Revise**: Review your will periodically, especially after significant life events such as marriage, divorce, birth of children, or changes in financial circumstances. Update your will as needed to reflect any changes in your wishes or circumstances.

Finalizing Your Will

7. **Execute Your Will**: Sign your will in the presence of witnesses as required by state law. Ensure that witnesses are impartial and not beneficiaries or heirs named in the will.

8. **Store Your Will Safely**: Store your original will in a secure location, such as a safe deposit box or fireproof safe, and inform your executors and trusted family members of its whereabouts. Consider providing copies to your executors and keeping a digital copy with your important documents.

9. **Inform Relevant Parties**: Inform your executors, beneficiaries, and other relevant parties about the existence and location of your will. Provide instructions on how to access your will in the event of your incapacity or death.

Additional Considerations

10. **Update Beneficiary Designations**: Review and update beneficiary designations on retirement accounts, life insurance policies, and other assets to ensure they align with your wishes as expressed in your will.

11. **Consider Trusts**: Evaluate whether establishing trusts may be beneficial for asset protection, tax planning, or providing for minor children or beneficiaries with special needs. Work with your attorney to determine the appropriate type of trust for your circumstances.

12. **Review Estate Tax Implications**: Consider the potential estate tax implications of your estate plan

and explore strategies for minimizing tax liabilities, such as gifting, charitable giving, or establishing trusts.

13. **Document Healthcare Directives**: Prepare advance directives, such as a living will and healthcare power of attorney, to outline your preferences for medical treatment and appoint a trusted individual to make healthcare decisions on your behalf if you become incapacitated.

CONCLUSION: SECURING YOUR LEGACY THROUGH THOUGHTFUL PLANNING

In the journey of life, we strive to build a legacy that transcends our existence—a testament to our values, aspirations, and the love we hold for those closest to us. Estate planning stands as the cornerstone of this endeavor, offering a roadmap to safeguard our assets, provide for our loved ones, and shape the future in accordance with our wishes. Throughout this book, we have embarked on a comprehensive exploration of estate planning, delving into its intricacies, challenges, and strategies for success. As we conclude this journey, let us reflect on the profound significance of estate planning and the transformative impact it holds for individuals, families, and communities.

Embracing the Essence of Estate Planning

At its core, estate planning is about much more than the distribution of assets upon death. It is a holistic process that encompasses a myriad of considerations, from healthcare directives and guardianship designations to tax planning strategies and philanthropic endeavors. By taking a proactive approach to estate planning, individuals can exert greater control over their affairs, minimize uncertainty, and provide clarity and direction to their loved ones during times of transition and loss.

Navigating the Complexities of Estate Planning

Estate planning is not without its complexities. From navigating intricate tax laws to managing family dynamics and addressing sensitive healthcare decisions, individuals face a multitude of challenges in crafting a comprehensive estate plan. Yet, armed with knowledge, foresight, and the guidance of experienced professionals, these challenges can be overcome. By understanding the nuances of estate planning and adopting a strategic approach to decision-making, individuals can maximize the effectiveness of their plans and achieve their long-term goals with confidence and certainty.

Strategies for Success in Estate Planning

Throughout this book, we have explored a myriad of strategies for success in estate planning, from setting clear goals and objectives to regularly reviewing and updating your plan to reflect changes in circumstances and preferences. We have delved into the importance of effective communication, collaboration with professionals, and staying informed about changes in laws and regulations that may impact your plan. By embracing these strategies and remaining vigilant to evolving circumstances, individuals can ensure that their estate plans remain relevant, effective, and aligned with their overarching objectives.

Preserving Your Legacy for Future Generations

At its essence, estate planning is about preserving a legacy— a legacy of love, wisdom, and generosity that endures long after we are gone. It is about empowering future generations to build upon the foundation we have laid, to pursue their dreams with confidence, and to make a positive impact on the world around them. Whether through philanthropy, education, or the preservation of family values, estate planning offers a means to shape the future and leave a lasting imprint on the world.

Conclusion: A Call to Action

As we bring our exploration of estate planning to a close, let us heed the call to action it represents. Let us commit to taking control of our financial affairs, protecting our loved ones, and preserving our legacy for generations to come. Let us embrace the opportunities that estate planning affords us to make a difference in the lives of those we hold dear and in the world at large. And let us remember that the true measure of our wealth lies not in the possessions we amass, but in the love we share, the values we uphold, and the impact we make on the world around us.

In closing, I extend my deepest gratitude to you, the reader, for embarking on this journey with me. May the insights gleaned from this book serve as a guiding light on your path to estate planning success, empowering you to secure your legacy and shape a future filled with hope, prosperity, and abundance.

www.ingramcontent.com/pod-product-compliance
Lightning Source LLC
Chambersburg PA
CBHW070434290526
45791CB00005B/1971